SandCastle™

Primeros Sonidos

I0880497

Ursula y Urbano

Cathy Camarena, M.Ed., and Gloria B. Ruff, M.Ed.

Consulting Editors

Lourdes Flores-Hanson, M.S.E., and Gloria Rosso-White

ABDO Publishing Company

capstone®

www.capstoneclassroom.com

Credits
Curriculum Coordinator: Nancy Tuminelly
Cover and Interior Design and Production: Mighty Media
Child Photography: Steven Wewerka, Wewerka Photography
Photo Credits: AbleStock, Comstock, Photodisc

ISBN 978-1-4966-0377-7 (paperback)

Printed in the United States of America in North Mankato, Minnesota.
072017 010637R

SandCastle™ books are created by a professional team of educators, reading specialists, and content developers around five essential components that include phonemic awareness, phonics, vocabulary, text comprehension, and fluency. All books are written, reviewed, and leveled for guided and early intervention reading, and designed for use in shared, guided, and independent reading and writing activities to support a balanced approach to literacy instruction.

SandCastle Level: Beginning

Uu

A B C Ch D E F G H

I J K L Ll M N Ñ O P

Q R S T U V W X Y Z

a b c ch d e f g h

i j k l ll m n ñ o p

q r s t u v w x y z

Ursula

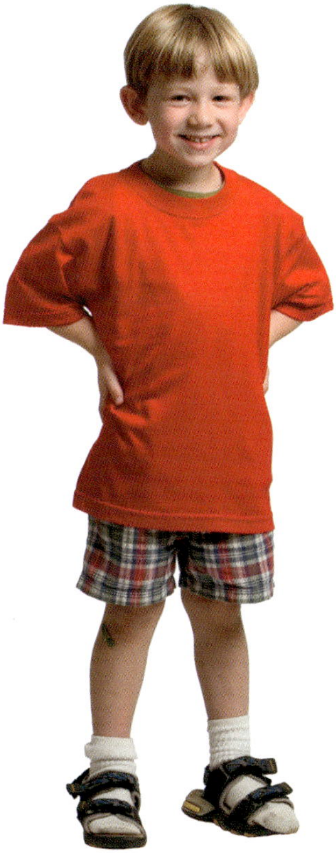

Urbano

uvas

ukelele

unicornio

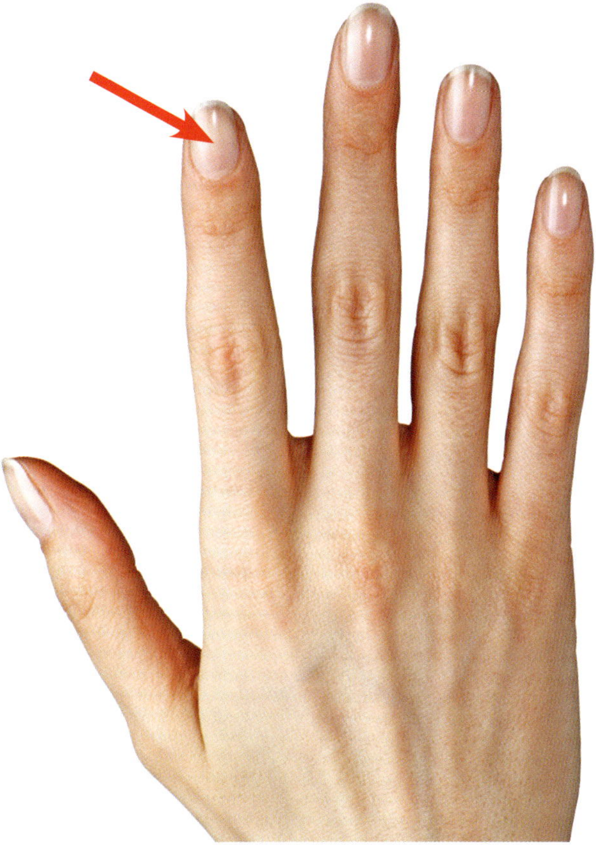

uña

1

uno

Las  son rojas.

Mira el .

El  es blanco.

Aquí hay una 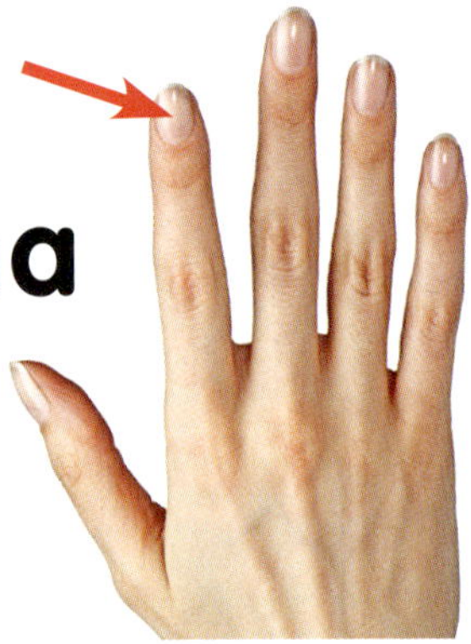 .

El 1 es negro.

Ursula tiene un unicornio.

A Ursula le gustan los unicornios.

Urbano tiene uvas.
Las uvas son rojas.

El unicornio es blanco.

El unicornio está encima de las uvas.

¿Cuáles de estas cosas comienzan con u?

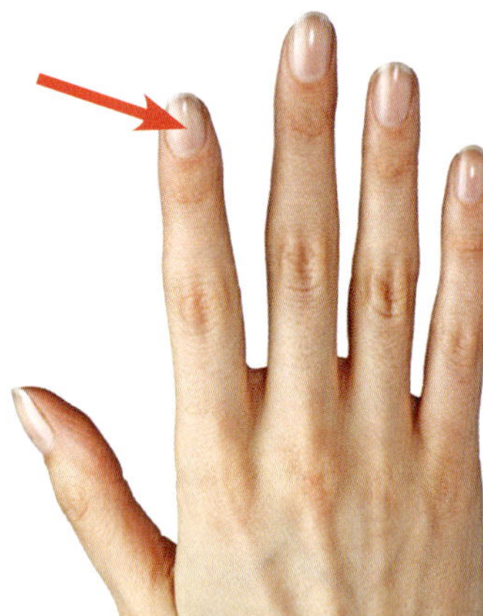

Más palabras que comienzan con u

11º

undécimo

uniforme

universidad

urraca

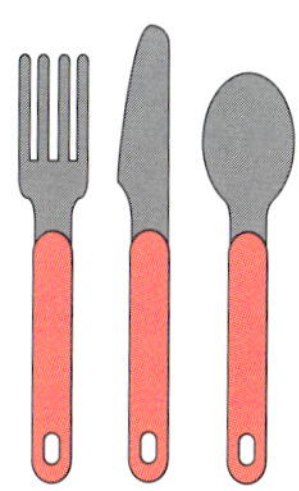

utensilios

About SandCastle™

A professional team of educators, reading specialists, and content developers created the SandCastle™ series to support young readers as they develop reading skills and strategies and increase their general knowledge. The SandCastle™ series has four levels that correspond to early literacy development in young children. The levels are provided to help teachers and parents select the appropriate books for young readers.

Emerging Readers
(no flags)

Beginning Readers
(1 flag)

Transitional Readers
(2 flags)

Fluent Readers
(3 flags)

These levels are meant only as a guide. All levels are subject to change.

ABDO Publishing Company
www.abdopub.com

capstone
www.capstoneclassroom.com